The Usborne
Cookbook
for Boys

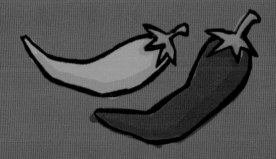

Photography by Howard Allman

Nutritional advice by Alison McLaughlin, MSc, RPHNutr

Digital imaging by Nick Wakeford

Edited by Jane Chisholm

Food preparation by Dagmar Vesely

The Usborne
Cookbook
for Boys

Abigail Wheatley

Designed and illustrated
by Erica Harrison

Recipes by
Catherine Atkinson

Contents

Getting started

Before you start cooking, it's a good idea to pick up a few basics, like how to measure and what equipment to use. You can read about these on the next few pages – then, get cooking!

When you're measuring, crouch down so the measurements are at eye level.

Get ready

Before you start cooking, read through the recipe to check you've got all the ingredients and equipment you need.

Clean up

Wash your hands. You should also wash fruit and vegetables, to remove any dirt or chemicals that might be on them. Rinse them under running water, or scrub to remove any stubborn dirt.

Weighing and measuring

When you're baking cakes or muffins, you need to measure accurately. With most other recipes, it doesn't matter so much.

Which weight?

All the weights in this book are listed both in metric (grams) and imperial (ounces and pounds). It's best not to switch between them in the middle of a recipe – stick to one or the other.

Tiny amounts

'A pinch' is the amount you can pick up between your thumb and first finger. This is often how you add salt and spices to recipes.

You can use measuring spoons, like these, or just use normal spoons.

If you want to be accurate, the ingredients should lie flat, not be heaped up.

Useful things to have in the kitchen...

Small sharp knife

Can opener

Saucepans – a large and a small one with matching lids are very handy

Mixing bowls

Spoons for measuring – if you don't have special measuring spoons, normal spoons are fine

Measuring jug

Wooden spoon

Potato masher

Lifter or spatula – for turning or lifting hot food

Oven gloves – to use when you handle anything hot

Garlic crusher

Chopping board – to keep food still while you chop it and protect kitchen surfaces

Lemon squeezer

Weighing scales

Ovenproof trays and dishes – a couple of different sized ones will be handy

Muffin tray or cake tin

Pastry brush – for brushing liquids onto foods

Grater with different sizes of holes

Vegetable peeler

Cling wrap, kitchen foil, kitchen paper, plastic food bags

Blender (optional)

Sieve or colander

Kebab skewers

Small jar with a tight-fitting lid

Rolling pin

Frying pan

Scissors

Useful things to know about this book...

How many?

The dishes in this book are for two people, except where it says otherwise. If you're cooking for one, halve all the amounts. If you're cooking for four, double them.

Chopping and changing

Apart from when you're baking cakes or muffins, you don't always have to follow the recipes in this book exactly. There are lots of suggestions for things to add and other ways to adapt them. Once you've got the hang of a recipe, you could try out your own ideas, too.

Oven shelves

All the oven-baked dishes in this book should be cooked in the middle of the oven. Arrange the oven shelves before you turn on the oven.

Salt...

Some of the recipes suggest adding a little salt. With others, you don't need to add any as there's enough in other ingredients, such as stock cubes or soy sauce.

Cooking times

Not all ovens are the same – so things may cook more quickly or slowly than the recipe says. Check the food is cooked before you eat it. The recipe will tell you how.

If you have a fan oven, shorten the cooking time or lower the temperature a little.

...and pepper

None of the recipes in this book is really hot, but some contain a little chilli or pepper. If you love hot food, you could add a little more – if you don't, reduce the amount or leave it out altogether.

Serving suggestions

Some of the recipes in this book are complete meals in themselves; others have suggestions for things that could be served with them. Look at 'Spuds on the side' and 'Veg on the side' for added inspiration (pages 36-39).

How to prepare some basic ingredients...

Onions

Cut the ends off the onion and peel off the skin. Cut the onion in half. Slice each half finely, then cut the slices into small pieces.

Spring onions

Trim off the hairy roots and most of the green part. Slice the rest.

Courgettes, carrots and cucumber

Trim off both ends, then chop into pieces.

Tomatoes

green core

Cut large tomatoes into quarters, then cut out the central green core from each quarter. Don't worry about the core in cherry tomatoes.

garlic
bulb

Garlic

To crush a clove of garlic, squeeze it in a garlic crusher. You'll get more from it if you peel off the papery skin first.

one
clove

Sweet peppers

Cut off the stalk and take out all the seeds before chopping.

Green beans

① ② ③

Trim off the hard end. Cut in half, if you like.

Avocado

1. Cut the avocado in half, running the knife around the hard central stone.
2. Scoop out the stone with a spoon and peel off all the skin.
3. Then, cut the flesh into chunks.

Peeling

Hold the fruit or vegetable in your hand and scrape it with a peeler again and again to remove all of the skin.

Grating

Most graters have big holes for coarse grating and small holes for fine grating. Choose the size of holes according to the recipe. Hold the food firmly and scrape it across the holes again and again. Don't scrape your fingers.

Some useful kitchen safety tips...

Protect yourself

When you're cooking, food and equipment can get very hot. Protect your hands with oven gloves, especially when you're getting things in and out of the oven.

Hot pans

Don't leave pan handles hanging over the front of the cooker – turn them to the side so you don't knock them off. Move hot pans carefully so you don't spill the contents.

Keep watch

Don't leave the kitchen while you've got anything cooking on the stove or under the grill. Make sure you remember to turn off the heat when you've finished cooking.

Meat safety

Raw meat, especially chicken, can contain nasty bacteria until it's been cooked. It's really important that you wash your hands – and any knives or chopping boards – as soon as you've finished handling raw meat.

Ask for help

If you're going to use special equipment such as a blender, or are trying out something new, make sure you know what you're doing. If in doubt, ask an adult to help.

Tidy up

It's a good idea to wipe up any spills on the floor, so you don't slip over on them. If you keep the kitchen fairly tidy as you cook, it will be easier to clean up afterwards.

Chop safely

When you're cutting with a sharp knife, always use a chopping board. Find out the best ways to cut courgettes, tomatoes and other vegetables on the page opposite.

Double-decker sandwich (page 12)

Dips and dippers (pages 18-19)

Baked potatoes (pages 24-25)

This section contains really quick and easy things to cook — from snacks and starters to main meals.

Easy bites

Sandwiches

All the sandwiches here are for one person. The fillings also work well in wraps or pitta breads, as well as sandwiches.

Cheese sandwich

Ingredients:

2 slices of bread

a little butter

a little mayonnaise

1 ripe tomato

a small piece of cucumber

a few slices of cheese such as Cheddar

a few lettuce leaves

① Spread one piece of bread with butter and the other with mayonnaise.

② Slice the tomato and cucumber. Put the cheese on one piece of bread, then top with the lettuce, tomato and cucumber.

③ Top with the second slice of bread. Then, cut your sandwich in half.

A double-decker sandwich

Double-decker sandwich

To make one double-decker sandwich, you'll need three slices of bread, some crispy bacon, lettuce, tomato and cooked chicken. Spread the bread with butter and mayo. Put lettuce, tomato and bacon on one slice of bread. Add another slice, then pile on lettuce and chicken and top with the final slice of bread.

Filling wraps

1. Lay out a soft tortilla or wrap. Spread over your chosen filling, leaving some room around the edges.

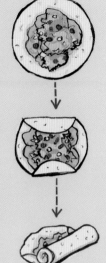

2. Fold over the top and bottom of the tortilla or wrap.

3. Roll up from one of the sides to enclose the filling. Then, cut it in half.

This wrap is filled with tuna mayo (page 15) with some added sweetcorn.

Other fillings to try...

...prawn mayo (page 25)
...smoked salmon and cream cheese
...guacamole (page 18) and cooked chicken
...cheese and onion (page 25)
...peanut butter and banana

Filling pittas

1. Toast a pitta bread (go to page 14 and follow the instructions for making toast). Leave it to cool for a minute or two, then cut it in half.

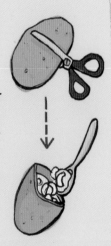

2. Open each half of the pitta bread into a pocket. Spoon in your chosen filling.

If you're using butter, it'll be easier to spread if you take it out of the fridge about 10 minutes before you start.

You could grind some pepper over savoury sandwich fillings.

13

Toast toppers

Making toast

Heat the grill to medium hot. Put the bread under the grill, about 5cm (2in) away from the heat. Toast for 1-2 minutes until golden brown, and the same for the other side.

The easiest way to make toast is using a pop-up toaster. But you'll need to use a grill if you want to add extra toppings, like the ones shown here.

Cheese on toast

Ingredients:

a chunk of cheese such as Cheddar (around 100g or 4oz)

2 slices of bread

Worcestershire sauce (optional)

② Grill for 2-3 minutes until bubbling. Season with a dash of Worcestershire sauce, if you like.

① Grate the cheese coarsely, then make your toast. When the toast is done, pile on the cheese.

Banana on toast

Ingredients:

1 ripe banana

2 slices of bread

2 tablespoons of plain fromage frais or yogurt

1 tablespoon of runny honey

① Slice the banana thickly, then toast the bread. Pile the banana onto the hot toast.

② Spoon over the fromage frais or yogurt, then drizzle over the honey. Grill for 2 minutes to warm everything through.

14

Tuna mayo melts

Ingredients:

a can of tuna (around 185g or 6½oz)

2 tablespoons of mayonnaise

2 tablespoons of plain yogurt

¼ of a red pepper

2 spring onions

2 slices of bread

2 large slices of cheese such as Cheddar

① Drain the tuna in a sieve. Then tip it into a bowl and break it up with a fork. Add the mayonnaise and yogurt and some pepper.

② Cut the red pepper into small pieces and add it to the tuna.

③ Slice the spring onions very finely. Add them to the tuna and mix well. This is your tuna mayo.

④ Toast your bread, then pile on the tuna mayo and top it with the cheese slices. Grill for 2-3 minutes, until the cheese is bubbling.

All these recipes are for one. The toppings also work really well on toasted English muffins, crumpets, slices of French bread or bagels.

Chef's tip:

Hot buttered toast is great with eggs. Cut it into strips to dip into soft-boiled eggs (page 16) for breakfast. Or pile scrambled eggs (page 17) onto toast for supper.

Tuna mayo melts — delicious served with a salad

Easy eggs

Eggs are the ultimate fast food, as they can easily be turned into quick and tasty meals. They're also used as an ingredient in lots of other recipes. Here you'll find out how to break and beat eggs, and how to cook them too.

Breaking an egg

1 Crack the shell by tapping it sharply on the edge of a bowl or mug.

2 Push your thumbs into the crack and pull the shell apart. Slide the egg gently into the bowl or mug.

Beating an egg

Use a fork.

Beat the white and the yolk until they are mixed together.

Chef's tips:

If you keep your eggs in the fridge, take them out about half an hour before you want to use them. Eggs at room temperature are better for cooking.

All the recipes in this book use medium sized eggs.

Boiling an egg

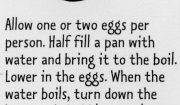

1 Allow one or two eggs per person. Half fill a pan with water and bring it to the boil. Lower in the eggs. When the water boils, turn down the heat, so it bubbles gently.

2 Cook the eggs for 5-6 minutes if you like firm whites and soft yolks – or a minute longer for large eggs. For hard-boiled eggs, cook for 9-10 minutes.

Scrambled eggs

Ingredients:

1-2 eggs per person

1 tablespoon of milk per person

a small chunk of butter

Scrambled eggs are great served on hot buttered toast (see page 14).

1. Break the eggs into a bowl. Add the milk and a little salt and pepper, then beat together with a fork.

Stir all the time.

2. Melt the butter in a pan over a low heat. Pour in the eggs. Stir for 2-3 minutes until the eggs set into fluffy clusters.

Before you start, you could prepare something extra to stir in when your eggs are scrambled, such as...

...a handful of grated cheese

...or a handful of chopped smoked salmon

...or 2 rashers of chopped or crumbled crispy bacon

Frying eggs

1. Allow one or two eggs per person. Pour a tablespoon of vegetable oil into a frying pan. Put it over a medium heat for a minute, then take it off.

2. Crack an egg, then hold it just above the pan and open the shell. Tip the egg into the oil, then put the pan back on the heat.

3. When the egg white starts to turn solid, spoon hot oil over the yolk. Fry the egg for 3-4 minutes, until cooked.

Dips and dippers

These dips and dippers are great for snacking, for serving alongside main courses, or for sharing with friends.

Ingredients:

Guacamole

1 ripe avocado

a clove of garlic

1/2 a lime

2 teaspoons of olive oil

1 tablespoon of plain or Greek yogurt

hot pepper sauce (optional)

(1) Cut the avocado in half and remove the stone, then peel off the skin and cut the flesh into chunks (see page 8).

(2) Tip into a bowl and mash roughly with a fork or a potato masher.

(3) Crush the garlic into the bowl. Squeeze the juice from the lime and add it, with the olive oil, yogurt and a few drops of hot pepper sauce. Mix together.

Tomato salsa

Ingredients:

3 ripe tomatoes

1/4 of a red onion or 1/2 a shallot

1/2 a lime

a few sprigs of fresh coriander or parsley (optional)

hot pepper sauce (optional)

If you can't get ripe tomatoes, make pineapple salsa instead. Drain a 225g (8oz) can of pineapple pieces and chop the pineapple finely. Add it at Step 1, instead of the tomatoes.

(1) Cut the tomatoes into small pieces and put them in a bowl. Chop the onion finely, then add that, too. Chop the coriander leaves finely and add to the bowl.

Leave at room temperature for 30 minutes to let the flavours mingle.

(2) Squeeze the juice from the lime and add it to the bowl with a few drops of hot pepper sauce. Mix well. The salsa will be chunky, not smooth – scoop it up with pitta strips or grilled tortilla chips (page 41).

Cucumber and yogurt dip

Ingredients:

a piece of cucumber around 5cm (2in) long

a sprig of fresh mint (optional)

1 small pot of plain or Greek yogurt (150ml or ¼ pint)

This dip is good as a side dish for the curry on pages 48-49. You could replace the mint with fresh coriander — this goes really well with curry.

1. Grate the cucumber coarsely. Put it in a sieve over a bowl and sprinkle over a pinch of salt — this will remove excess juices.

2. Chop the mint leaves finely. Squeeze out the cucumber and put it into a clean bowl with the mint and yogurt. Mix everything together.

Crunchy dippers

Ingredients:

2 pitta breads

a piece of cucumber around 8cm (3in) long

1 small carrot

1 small red pepper

a handful of cherry tomatoes

Dips and dippers make perfect party food.

1. Toast the pitta breads in a pop-up toaster, or grill them, following the instructions for toast on page 14. Then, cut them into strips.

2. Cut the cucumber, carrot and pepper into chunky sticks. Put them on a plate with the tomatoes, pitta strips and dips.

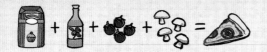

Pizza

Ingredients:

Tomato Sauce

1 onion (optional)

2 tablespoons of olive oil

a clove of garlic

1 can of chopped tomatoes (400g or 14oz)

2 tablespoons of tomato purée

1 teaspoon of dried mixed herbs

Pizza base

110g (4oz) self-raising flour

¼ teaspoon of baking powder

5 tablespoons of milk

a little olive oil

Topping

75g (3oz) mozzarella

① Heat the oven to 200°C, 400°F or gas mark 6. Follow the tomato sauce recipe on page 32. Then, put the flour, baking powder and a pinch of salt into a bowl and mix.

② Make a hollow in the middle. Put the milk and 2 teaspoons of olive oil in a jug. Pour them into the hollow. Mix to make a soft dough.

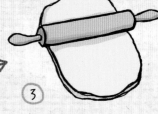

③ Sprinkle a work surface with flour, then shape the dough into a ball with your hands. Roll it out into a circle or rectangle around 1cm (½in) thick.

④ Spread a little oil over a baking tray using kitchen paper. Lift on the dough and spread on half the tomato sauce (save the rest for later).

⑤ Drain the liquid from the mozzarella and chop it into thin slices. Scatter them on and add any other toppings you like.

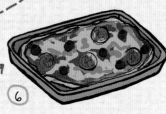

⑥ Bake in the oven for 20 minutes, or until the base is risen and golden and the cheese is bubbling.

You could try these pizza toppings...

Sliced pepperoni and black olives

Halved cherry tomatoes

Basil leaves

Try another cheese instead of mozzarella.

Sliced mushrooms and ham

Chopped peppers

Pasta

Pasta is really quick and easy. These pages show you how to cook different types and make some simple sauces, too. You'll also find step-by-step instructions for other pasta sauces on pages 32-33.

pages 32-33

Ingredients:

Cooking spaghetti

150g (5oz) dried spaghetti

half a teaspoon of olive oil

Chef's tips:

You can cook most types of dried pasta in the same way as spaghetti. Find cooking times on the packet.

To check if pasta is cooked, lift out a piece, rinse it under cold water and bite it. It should be tender but not soggy.

One of the simplest ways to serve pasta is with grated cheese. Stir around 25g (1oz) into freshly cooked pasta with a little salt and pepper.

Half-fill a large saucepan with water and put it over a high heat until it boils. Turn down the heat so it bubbles gently, then add the oil and a pinch of salt.

1

2

Hold the spaghetti in a bunch at one end and put the other end into the water. Press the spaghetti into the water as it softens, then use a spoon to push in the ends. Give it a stir.

3

Boil for around 10-12 minutes (follow the times printed on the packet). When the pasta is cooked, drain it in a colander, then tip it back into the pan. Add your chosen sauce and stir.

Tuna tomato pasta

Scatter over a little chopped fresh parsley or other herbs, if you have some.

Ingredients:

150g (5oz) dried pasta such as penne

a small can of tuna (around 100g or 4oz)

around 6 cherry tomatoes

3 tablespoons of cream cheese or mascarpone cheese

Put the pasta on to boil. Drain the tuna and put it in a pan with the halved tomatoes and some pepper. Add the cream cheese and heat gently until it melts and the tomatoes are soft. Stir it into your cooked, drained pasta.

Spicy sausage pasta

Ingredients:

150g (5oz) dried pasta such as fusilli

100g (4oz) spicy sausage such as chorizo

2 teaspoons of olive oil

a clove of garlic

a small pinch of dried chilli flakes

Or you could try...

...replacing the sausage with the same amount of chopped mushrooms or drained, tinned chickpeas.

...leaving out the sausage to make a spicy chilli and garlic sauce.

① Put your pasta on to boil. While it's cooking, cut the sausage into pieces, and put them into a small pan with the olive oil.

② Cook over a medium heat for 3-4 minutes, until the sausage is sizzling. Crush the garlic into the pan and stir in the chilli flakes.

③ Cook for a few seconds, then turn off the heat. Stir it into your cooked, drained pasta.

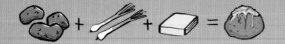

Baked potatoes and fillings

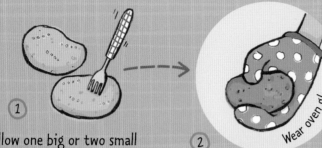

1

Allow one big or two small potatoes per person. Heat the oven to 180°C, 350°F or gas mark 4. Prick the potatoes all over with a fork and put them on a baking tray.

2

Wear oven gloves.

Bake for 1 hour. Then, take the potatoes out of the oven and squeeze them gently. If they feel soft, they are ready; if not, bake them for another 15 minutes.

3

When they are ready, cut a cross in the top of each one and add one of the following fillings.

Ingredients:

Coleslaw

a small piece of white cabbage (around 100g or 4oz)

1 small apple

1 tablespoon of lemon juice

1 small carrot

2 spring onions

2 tablespoons of mayonnaise

2 tablespoons of plain or Greek yogurt

1

Put the cabbage on a board and carefully cut out the hard stem with a sharp knife. Slice the rest of the cabbage finely.

Make sure the knife is facing away from you.

2

Cut the apple in half, then into quarters. Cut out the cores. Grate the apple coarsely. Then put it in a bowl with the lemon juice and mix.

3

Grate the carrot coarsely and chop the spring onions finely. Add them to the bowl, with the cabbage, mayonnaise, yogurt and a little salt and pepper. Mix well.

Cheese and onion

Ingredients:

a chunk of cheese such as Cheddar
(around 100g or 4oz)

2 spring onions

 Use the
big holes.

Grate the cheese coarsely and chop the spring
onions finely. Put everything in a bowl and add
a little pepper. Mix together.

Jacket potatoes are simple, tasty
and good for you, too.

Prawn mayo

Ingredients:

1 teaspoon of tomato purée

1 teaspoon of lemon juice

1 tablespoon of mayonnaise

1 tablespoon of plain or Greek
yogurt

hot pepper sauce (optional)

100g (4oz) peeled, cooked prawns

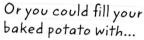

Or you could fill your baked potato with...

...Bolognese sauce (page 33)

...tomato sauce (page 32)

...tuna mayo (page 15)

...guacamole (page 18)

...chilli con carne (pages 40-41)

...plain grated cheese

① Put the tomato purée, lemon juice,
mayonnaise, yogurt and a few drops
of hot pepper sauce into a bowl.

② Add a little salt and pepper
and mix well. Then, add the
prawns and stir them in, too.

If you need to
defrost frozen prawns
in a hurry, put them in a
jug of cold water for a few
minutes, or put them in a
sieve and rinse them under
the cold tap. Then, pat them
dry with kitchen paper.

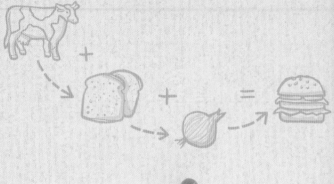

Hamburger (pages 44-45)

Fish pie (pages 30-31)

The section contains lots of tasty and filling main courses, with suggestions of what to serve with them.

Bolognese sauce (page 33)

Main meals

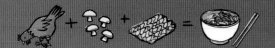

One-pot noodles

Ingredients:

4 spring onions

1 red or yellow pepper

2 skinless, boneless chicken breasts or thighs

1 lemon

1 chicken or vegetable stock cube

1 tablespoon of sunflower oil

a clove of garlic

a pinch of chilli flakes

a pinch of sugar

1 tablespoon of soy sauce

100g (4oz) fine egg noodles

1. This dish cooks really quickly, so you'll need to prepare all the ingredients first.

2. Chop the spring onion into small pieces and cut the pepper and chicken into bite-sized chunks.

Use the small holes.

3. Grate the lemon finely, until you have about a teaspoon of rind. Then, squeeze out the juice.

4. Put the stock cube into a jug. Add 250ml (9floz) boiling water and stir until it dissolves.

Stir all the time.

5. Heat the oil in a large pan over a medium heat for about a minute. Add the chicken and spring onions and cook for 2-3 minutes, until the chicken is white all over.

You could add different vegetables. Sprinkle some chopped fresh coriander over the finished dish too, if you like.

⑥ Add the pepper and cook for one more minute. Crush the garlic into the pan. Cook for a few more seconds.

⑦ Pour in the stock, lemon rind and juice, chilli flakes, sugar and soy sauce.

Chef's tips:

You could replace the chicken with a small packet of prawns — add them at Step 7.

Instead of the lemon, use 2 limes.

You could add some sliced baby corn and mushrooms at Step 7.

Leave a small gap.

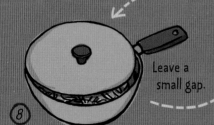

⑧ When the mixture boils, turn down the heat so it just bubbles. Put a lid on the pan and cook for 2 more minutes.

⑨ Break each block of noodles in half. Add to the pan and stir. When the mixture is bubbling again, put the lid back on as before and cook for 3 minutes.

⑩ Test the noodles and vegetables; when they are tender, you're ready to eat.

Fish pie

Ingredients:

Mash topping

350g (12oz) potatoes

10g ($^1/_2$oz) butter

2 tablespoons of milk

Fish filling

100g (4oz) cream cheese or mascarpone cheese

150g (5oz) skinless, boneless white fish, such as cod or haddock

100g (4oz) raw, peeled king prawns

3 spring onions

Fish pie is good with peas. Cook them from frozen according to the instructions on the packet.

① Heat your oven to 180°C, 350°F or gas mark 4. Follow the recipe on page 37 for mashed potatoes. While the potatoes are cooking, make the pie filling.

② Cut the spring onions into small pieces, and put them into an ovenproof pie dish.

Cottage pie

You could make a cottage pie using the Bolognese sauce on page 33. Put it in a pie dish and top with mashed potato. Bake for 25 minutes.

These individual cottage pies were baked in little ovenproof dishes.

③ Cut the fish into bite-sized chunks, then add to the pie dish with the prawns.

④ Add the cream cheese or mascarpone and some salt and pepper and mix gently.

⑤ Spread the mashed potato over the top. Put the dish on an oven tray and bake in the oven for 35 minutes.

⑥ Check that the fish is flaky and white, and the prawns are pink. If not, bake for another 10-15 minutes.

Chef's tips:

You could add extra ingredients to the filling, such as...
...a handful of fresh parsley
...a chopped hard-boiled egg
...a handful of frozen peas.

Try using a mixture of fish such as salmon and smoked fish.

You'll probably have some cream cheese or mascarpone left over. You could use it to make the trifle on pages 62-63.

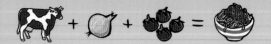

Simple sauces

These sauces are great for eating with pasta, but that's not all. The tomato sauce also doubles up as a topping for pizza (pages 20-21) and cannelloni (see below). And you can use the Bolognese to make cottage pies, too (see page 31).

Ingredients:

Tomato sauce

1 onion

1 tablespoon of olive oil

a clove of garlic

1 can of chopped tomatoes (400g or 14oz)

2 tablespoons of tomato purée

1 teaspoon of dried mixed herbs

Stir occasionally.

1 Chop the onion finely. Heat the oil in a saucepan over a medium heat for a minute. Then, add the onion and cook for 5 minutes.

2 Crush the garlic into the pan. Cook for 1–2 more minutes, stirring all the time, until the onion is soft.

3 Add the tomatoes, tomato purée, herbs and a little salt and pepper. When the sauce boils, turn down the heat so it just bubbles. Cook for 25 minutes.

Cannelloni with tomato sauce

Cannelloni

Try using the tomato sauce to make cannelloni. Turn the oven to 180°C, 350°F or gas mark 4. Stuff 6 cannelloni pasta tubes with herb-flavoured soft cheese, using the thin end of a spoon. You could add a handful of boiled spinach leaves too, if you like. Put in a heatproof dish and cover with tomato sauce. Bake for 30-40 minutes.

Bolognese sauce

Ingredients:

1 onion

1 tablespoon of olive oil

a clove of garlic

225g (8oz) lean minced beef

1 beef stock cube

1 can of chopped tomatoes (400g or 14oz)

2 tablespoons of tomato purée

1 teaspoon of dried mixed herbs

1 Follow steps 1-2 of the tomato sauce recipe opposite.

2 Then, add the beef to the pan and cook it for about 10 minutes, until it's brown all over. Break up any lumps with a spoon.

Keep stirring.

3 Put the stock cube into a jug. Pour on 300ml (½ pint) boiling water and stir until it dissolves. Then, add it to the pan.

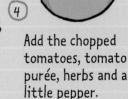

4 Add the chopped tomatoes, tomato purée, herbs and a little pepper.

Stir occasionally.

5 When the sauce boils, turn down the heat so it just bubbles. Put on a lid, leaving a small gap, and cook for 30 minutes. Then, take off the lid and cook for 10 more minutes.

Serve with cooked spaghetti (page 22) and scatter with freshly grated Parmesan cheese for the classic spaghetti Bolognese.

Spaghetti with Bolognese sauce

Easy roast chicken

Ingredients:

1 red onion

350g (12oz) potatoes

1 carrot

a little olive oil

4 chicken thighs or drumsticks

1 lemon

1 courgette

a clove of garlic

1 lemon

2 sprigs of fresh rosemary or other fresh herbs (optional)

Use oven gloves.

① Heat the oven to 200°C, 400°F or gas mark 6 and put a roasting tin in the oven. Cut the onion into wedges and put them in a bowl.

② Cut the potatoes and carrot into bite-sized chunks. Put them in the bowl and add a tablespoon of olive oil. Mix everything together.

③ Take the tin out of the oven and spread out the vegetables in it. Put the chicken on top and add a little salt and pepper. Bake for 20 minutes.

Use oven gloves.

④ Cut the courgette into bite-sized chunks. Put them in bowl with a tablespoon of olive oil. Crush in the garlic and mix. Then, cut the lemon into wedges.

⑤ Take the tray out of the oven. Lift off the chicken and add the courgettes, lemon and rosemary. Turn everything over. Put the chicken back on top and bake for 20-25 minutes.

⑥ Then, cut into a piece of chicken – it should be white inside. If any pink shows, cook for 10 more minutes, then test again.

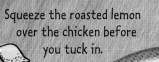
Squeeze the roasted lemon over the chicken before you tuck in.

The rosemary adds lots of flavour during cooking, but don't eat it as it tastes bitter.

If you like peppers, you could try adding some sliced red or yellow ones at Step 4.

You could replace the chicken with fish, such as salmon fillets. Lay them on top of the vegetables at Step 5.

Spuds on the side

New potatoes are small and firm, and are great for boiling and salads. 'Old' potatoes are larger. They go fluffy when they're cooked, so they're ideal for mashing and baking (see pages 24–25 for baked potatoes).

Potato salad with lemon mayo dressing

Ingredients:

Boiled new potatoes

350g (12oz) new potatoes

a small chunk of butter

1. Put the potatoes into a pan of cold water with a pinch of salt and put it over a medium heat until it boils. Reduce the heat so it boils gently.

2. Put a lid on, leaving a small gap, and cook for 15–20 minutes. Test a potato by cutting into it. If it's soft, it's ready.

3. When the potatoes are cooked, drain them in a colander. Serve hot, topped with a little butter.

Potato salad

Boil some new potatoes, following Steps 1–2 on the left. When the potatoes are cooked, drain them and leave them to cool.

Meanwhile, chop 2 spring onions finely and make the lemon mayo dressing from page 39.
Cut the cooled potatoes into bite-sized chunks.
Put everything into a bowl and mix gently.

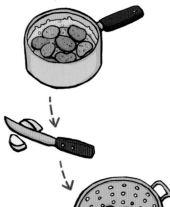

Ingredients:

Mashed potatoes

350g (12oz) 'old' potatoes

10g (1/2oz) butter

2 tablespoons of milk

You could add these to your mashed potatoes...

...a tablespoon of wholegrain mustard

...or a handful of chopped fresh herbs such as chives or parsley

...or a handful of grated cheese such as Cheddar

1 If you want a really smooth mash, peel the potatoes. Cut out any spots, then cut the potatoes into chunks.

2 Cook the potatoes, following Steps 1-2 opposite.

3 Drain the cooked potates, then tip them back into the pan. Add the butter, milk and a little salt and pepper. Mash until no lumps are left.

Ingredients:

Homemade oven chips

350g (12oz) 'old' potatoes

1 tablespoon of cooking oil, such as sunflower oil

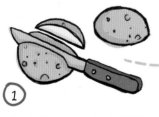

1 Heat the oven to 200°C, 400°F or gas mark 6. Cut the potatoes into chunky slices, then into fat chip shapes.

2 Spoon the oil onto a baking tray and add the chips. Mix them with your hands to coat them in the oil.

3 Every 15 minutes or so, take the tray out and turn the chips. Check to see how they are cooking – they are done when they're soft in the middle and golden brown. This should take around 40-45 minutes.

Veg on the side

Whether you boil them, grill them or put them in a salad, vegetables can turn a simple dish into a proper meal. And if there are some you don't like, use others – there are plenty to choose from.

Boiling veg

Boiling is a quick and easy way to cook veg such as carrots, peas, green beans and broccoli. Allow a handful of veg per person, as a side dish.

① Prepare the veg, following the instructions on page 8. Cut any large veg into bite-sized chunks.

② Fill a pan with water and heat it until it boils. Lower in the veg. Turn down the heat so the water boils gently and put on a lid, leaving a small gap.

③ Cook for around 8-12 minutes, or until the veg are tender but not soggy. Drain them in a colander.

Roasted vegetables

Grilling and roasting veg

On page 47, you can find out how to make grilled veggie kebabs. If you dont have any skewers, just cut the veg into strips and grill them in the grill pan.

Try roasting veg, too. Follow the recipe for Easy roast chicken on pages 34-35, but just leave out the chicken. Add some tomatoes and peppers too, if you like.

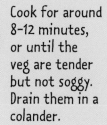

Salads

Salads don't just mean lettuce. You could make potato salad (see page 36) or coleslaw (page 24). Or try these ideas:

Tomato salad: chop a small piece of red onion finely. Chop three large tomatoes or 12 cherry tomatoes. Dress with the honey mustard dressing below.

Tuna salad: hard-boil an egg (page 16). Boil some new potatoes (page 36) and green beans (opposite). When they're cool, peel and chop the egg and chop the veg. Add lettuce, tomatoes, olives and a drained can of tuna. Dress with either of the dressings below.

Tuna salad with honey mustard dressing

Honey mustard dressing

Ingredients:

2 tablespoons of olive oil

2 teaspoons of lemon juice or your favourite vinegar

1/2 teaspoon of wholegrain mustard

1/2 teaspoon of runny honey

Take a small jar with a tight-fitting lid. Put in all the ingredients and a little salt and pepper. Put on the lid and shake well.

Lemon mayo dressing

Ingredients:

2 tablespoons of mayonnaise

2 tablespoons of plain or Greek yogurt

2 teaspoons of lemon juice

Put all the ingredients in a small bowl with a pinch of salt and pepper. Mix well.

Chilli con carne

Ingredients:

- 1 red onion
- 1 red pepper
- 2 tablespoons of olive oil
- a clove of garlic
- 2-3 teaspoons of mild chilli powder or 2-3 pinches of chilli flakes
- 1 teaspoon of ground cumin

- 450g (1lb) lean minced beef
- 1 beef or vegetable stock cube
- 1 can of chopped tomatoes (400g or 14oz)
- 1 tablespoon of tomato purée
- 1 can of red kidney beans (400g or 14oz)
- 1 teaspoon of cocoa powder or 2 squares of plain chocolate (optional)

This recipe serves four – save half of it for the next day if there are only two of you.

(1) Chop the onion finely and cut the pepper into small pieces.

(2) Put the oil in a large pan and add the pepper and onion. Cook over a medium heat for 5 minutes, stirring often.

(3) Crush the garlic into the pan. Add the chilli and cumin. Cook for a minute, stirring all the time.

(4) Add the beef to the pan and cook it for about 10 minutes, stirring until it's brown all over. Break up any lumps with the spoon.

(5) Put the stock cube into a heatproof jug. Add 150ml (½ pint) of boiling water, and stir until it's dissolved.

(6) Stir every now and then.

Add the stock to the pan, along with the tomatoes and tomato purée. Heat until it boils, then turn down the heat so it just bubbles. Put a lid on the pan, leaving a small gap. Cook for 15 minutes.

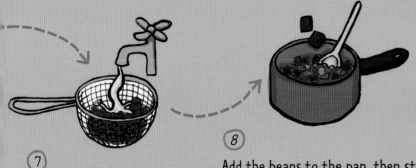

⑦ Tip the red kidney beans into a sieve or colander and rinse well.

⑧ Add the beans to the pan, then stir in the cocoa powder or chocolate. Simmer without a lid for another 15 minutes.

Chef's tips:

The chocolate doesn't make the chilli sweet, it just adds flavour.

For a bean chilli, leave out the beef and add a drained and rinsed can of mixed beans at Step 7.

Chilli con carne is delicious with a little grated cheese, some grilled tortilla chips and a bowl of guacamole (page 18).

(page 18).

Ingredients:

Grilled tortilla chips

1 soft corn or flour tortilla per person
1 teaspoon of olive oil per person

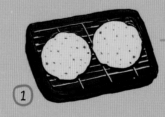

① Turn the grill to a medium heat. Brush both sides of the tortillas with oil and put them on a grill pan. Grill for 1-2 minutes, then turn and cook for 1 minute.

② Leave the tortillas for a minute, to cool and crisp up. Then, cut each tortilla into 8 chips.

Rapid rice

Rice makes a great side dish for things like curry, chilli con carne and kebabs, but you can also use it in main dishes. These pages show you how to boil and steam rice, and how to make a quick and tasty rice dish called jambalaya.

Boiling rice

Allow around 75-100g (3-4oz) of rice per person.

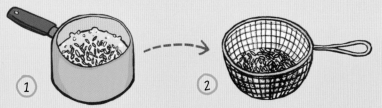

1. Half-fill a pan with water. Heat the water until it boils, then add the rice to the pan.

2. When the water boils, turn down the heat so it bubbles gently. Cook for as long as it says on the packet. Then, drain the rice in a sieve.

Chef's tips:

There are lots of different kinds of rice, but most have cooking instructions printed on the packet.

The simplest rice to cook is called 'easy-cook'. It's treated to stop the grains sticking together.

If you're cooking rice that's not easy-cook, you may need to rinse or soak it first — see what it says on the packet.

Steaming rice

1. Measure one cup (half a mug) of rice and two cups (one mug) of water per person into a pan. Heat until the water boils.

2. Stir, then turn down the heat a little. Put on a lid and cook for as long as it says on the packet. If any water is left at the end, cook for another minute or two.

If your cooked rice looks sticky, tip it into a sieve and rinse it with boiling water.

Once you've cooked rice, it's best to eat it straight away, as it can go bad very quickly.

42

Jambalaya

Ingredients:

175g (6oz) easy-cook rice

150g (5oz) spicy sausage such as chorizo

1 red pepper

1 onion

a clove of garlic

1 tablespoon of olive oil

a large pinch of ground ginger

1/2 teaspoon of mild chilli powder or a small pinch of chilli flakes

2 teaspoons of tomato purée

100g (4oz) cooked peeled prawns

1

Cook the rice by following the steps opposite. Meanwhile, chop the sausage and pepper into bitesized chunks. Chop the onion finely.

2

Put the oil into a large pan and heat it over a medium heat for about 30 seconds. Add the chorizo and cook for 4-5 minutes.

3

Add the onion and crush the garlic into the pan. Cook for 4 minutes. Then add the pepper and cook for 4 more minutes.

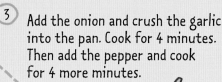

Stir often.

4

Stir in the ginger and chilli and cook for another minute, until the peppers soften. Then stir in 2 tablespoons of water, a little salt and pepper, the tomato purée and the prawns.

5

Turn the heat down low and put on a lid. Cook for 3-4 minutes until everything is piping hot.

You could add a sliced, uncooked chicken breast at Step 2 and a handful frozen peas at Step 4.

Hamburgers

Ingredients:

a little olive oil

1 slice of bread (about 25g or 1oz)

a large pinch of dried mixed herbs

2 tablespoons of milk

1 teaspoon of soy sauce or Worcestershire sauce

½ a red onion

225g (8oz) lean minced beef

1

Heat the oven to 200°C, 400°F or gas mark 6. Then, spread a little oil over a baking tray using a piece of kitchen paper.

2

Tear the bread into small pieces. Put them in a bowl with the herbs, then sprinkle over the milk and soy or Worcestershire sauce.

3

Leave to soak for 2-3 minutes, then mash roughly with a fork.

Serve your hamburger in a bun with salad and some tomato salsa (page 18).

You could cook some homemade chips in the oven with your hamburgers. Put them in around 10 minutes before the burgers — see page 37.

Meatballs

To make meatballs, follow the recipe below, but at Step 5, shape the mixture into 10 small meatballs. Bake in the oven for 15 minutes, turning often, until brown. Serve with spaghetti and tomato sauce (page 32).

Meatballs with spaghetti and tomato sauce

4

Chop the onion finely and add it to the bread. Then, add the beef and a little salt and pepper.

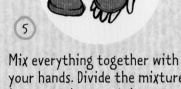

5

Mix everything together with your hands. Divide the mixture into two pieces and shape them into burgers.

6

Put the burgers onto the baking tray. Cook them in the oven for 10 minutes.

You could add extra flavours to your burgers, such as...

...a teaspoon of mustard or a crushed clove of garlic at Step 4

...or a pinch of chilli flakes at Step 2

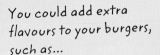

Wear oven gloves.

7

Lift out the baking tray, turn the burgers over and cook them for 10 more minutes. Then, check to see if they are cooked.

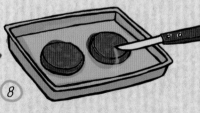

8

Push a knife into a burger, then press on the top. The juices that run out should be clear, not pink. If they are pink, bake for 10 more minutes, then test again.

Barbecue dippers

These tasty chicken and veggie dippers are served with a delicious barbecue dipping sauce. You can grill the dippers, or even cook them on a barbecue.

Ingredients:

Barbecue sauce

2 teaspoons of sunflower oil

2 tablespoons of tomato purée

1 tablespoon of balsamic vinegar

1 tablespoon of Worcestershire sauce

2 tablespoons of runny honey

hot pepper sauce sauce (optional)

a clove of garlic

5 tablespoons of apple juice

(1) Put the oil, tomato purée, vinegar, Worcestershire sauce, honey and a few drops of hot pepper sauce into a small pan. Crush in the garlic and mix.

(2) Spoon a little of the mixture into two small bowls.

You'll need these for brushing onto your chicken and the vegetables, before you cook them.

(3) Next, stir the fruit juice into the pan. Cook over a low heat for 10 minutes. This is your dipping sauce.

Chicken drumsticks

Allow two chicken drumsticks per person.

(1) Turn the grill to a medium temperature. Cut two or three slashes through the skin of each drumstick.

(2) Take one bowl of the mixture you set aside, and brush it over the chicken. Grill the chicken for 15–20 minutes, turning often, until it's brown all over.

(3) Check the chicken is cooked by piercing to the middle with a sharp knife or skewer. The juices that run out should be clear, not pink. Serve with the dipping sauce.

You could try...

...adding cherry tomatoes to your veggie kebabs.

...serving your dippers with toasted pitta breads and coleslaw (see page 24).

...replacing the chicken with sausages — cook under a medium hot grill for 12-15 minutes, turning often.

Veggie kebabs

Ingredients:

1 red onion

1 courgette

1 red or yellow pepper

8 small mushrooms

1 You'll need 4 kebab skewers. If they're wooden, put them in a dish of water for half an hour. This will stop them burning.

2 Chop the courgette and pepper into bite-sized chunks. Cut the onion into quarters, then cut across each quarter. Push all the vegetables onto the skewers.

3 Heat the grill to medium hot. Take one bowl of the mixture you set aside, and brush it all over the vegetables.

4 Grill the kebabs for 10 minutes. Turn them over, then cook for another 5-10 minutes. Serve with the dipping sauce.

5 To eat a kebab, hold the skewer upright with the point on your plate. Pull the veggies off with a fork.

Lamb curry

Ingredients:

2 large lamb steaks (around 350g or 12oz total weight)

1 vegetable stock cube

1 onion

2 tablespoons of sunflower oil

1 small sweet potato (around 175g or 6oz)

1 teaspoon of ground turmeric

1 teaspoon of mild chilli powder or a pinch of chilli flakes

2 teaspoons of ground cumin

4 teaspoons of ground coriander

2 cloves of garlic

4 tablespoons of tomato purée

1 small can of chickpeas (200g or 7oz)

1 small pot of plain or Greek yogurt (150ml or ¼ pint)

a handful of fresh coriander (optional)

easy-cook basmati rice

This curry is for four people – if there are only two of you, save half for the next day.

① Cut the lamb into bitesized chunks. Put the stock cube into a jug. Pour on 200ml (7floz) boiling water and stir until it dissolves.

② Chop the onion finely. Put it in a large saucepan with the oil over a medium heat and cook for 7-8 minutes.

③ Turn up the heat a little. Add the meat and fry for 2-3 minutes, turning the pieces so they brown all over.

Stir all the time.

④ Chop the sweet potato into small chunks. Add to the pan along with the turmeric, chilli powder, cumin and ground coriander.

⑤ Crush in the garlic and stir in the tomato purée, then add the stock.

⑥ Heat until it boils, then turn down the heat so it bubbles gently. Cover the pan with a lid, leaving a small gap. Cook for 15 minutes.

Stir from time to time.

The yogurt and cucumber dip on page 19 makes a tasty side dish for this curry.

You could add a handful of green beans to the curry at Step 7, if you like.

⑦ Drain and rinse the chickpeas and add them to the curry.

⑧ Stir in the yogurt. Then, cook with the lid off for 15 minutes.

It may look a little grainy, but don't worry - this is normal.

⑨ Meanwhile, cook the rice following the instructions on page 42.

⑩ While the rice is cooking, test the vegetables with knife. If they're still hard, cook for 10 more minutes.

⑪ When the curry is cooked, sprinkle on the fresh coriander and serve with the rice.

You could also try...

...using chicken breasts instead of the lamb.

...leaving out the meat for a vegetable curry — just double the amount of sweet potato and chickpeas and double the amount of water in the stock.

Chocolate biscuit cake (pages 54-55)

This section contains delicious drinks, great puddings and sweet snacks.

Banana and berry smoothies (pages 52-53)

Apple pie (pages 58-59)

Sweet treats

Smoothies and shakes

Blitz it up...

If you have a blender, you can make the recipes on this page really quickly. Remove any stalks or thick skin from the fruit. Then put all the ingredients in the blender and blitz. Or follow the steps below...

Banana smoothie

Ingredients:

1 banana

5 tangerines or a small glass of orange juice

1 teaspoon of runny honey

Makes one smoothie

① Peel the banana and mash it with a fork or a potato masher, until it's smooth.

② Squeeze the juice from the tangerines, if you're using them. Add the tangerine or orange juice and the honey to the banana. Mix until the drink is smooth and frothy.

A banana smoothie and a berry smoothie

Berry smoothie

Ingredients:

a large handful of mixed berries, such as blueberries, raspberries and strawberries

a small glass of apple juice

1 teaspoon of runny honey

Makes one smoothie

① Remove any stalks from the fruit. Then mash with a fork or a masher until it's fairly smooth.

② Add the apple juice and honey, then mix until the drink is smooth and frothy.

Chef's tip:

The fruit will mash easily if it's ripe. But if you like your smoothies really smooth, push the mashed fruit through a sieve.

Chocolate milkshake

Ingredients:

a glass of chilled milk

a scoop of chocolate frozen yogurt or ice cream

Makes one milkshake

 = Chocolate milkshake

Beat the frozen yogurt or ice cream into the milk with a fork. It's ready when the drink is smooth and frothy.

You can make any flavour of milkshake you like, using different types of ice cream or frozen yogurt.

Chocolate biscuit cake

Ingredients:

200g (7oz) plain chocolate

85g (3½oz) butter

1 tablespoon of golden syrup

6 plain biscuits (around 100g or 4oz)

a handful of raisins

a handful of unsalted, shelled nuts such as hazelnuts or almonds

This recipe makes lots — share it with some friends.

Try out different combinations of fruit and nuts — such as dried apricots with glacé cherries and pistachios.

① Take a cake tin or plastic box around 18cm (7in) wide. Line it with baking parchment or kitchen foil.

② Pour some water into a pan, so it's around 3cm (1in) deep. Heat until the water bubbles, then turn off the heat.

③ Break the chocolate into chunks and cut up the butter. Put them into a heatproof bowl with the golden syrup.

Or you could...

...replace the raisins with glacé cherries or dried fruit such as apricots, cherries, cranberries, dates, figs or mangoes.

...use almonds, pecans, peanuts, pistachios or macadamia nuts.

...replace the biscuits with the same amount of cornflakes, muesli or mini marshmallows.

...use milk chocolate instead of plain — but don't use white chocolate as it won't set properly.

④ Put the bowl into the pan and leave it for a minute or two.

Wear oven gloves.

⑤ Stir the chocolate and butter until they have melted. Then, lift the bowl out of the pan.

⑥ Put the biscuits into a plastic food bag and tie up the top. Roll a rolling pin on it to break the biscuits into chunks.

⑦ Add the biscuits to the bowl along with the raisins and nuts. Stir everything together.

⑧ Spoon the mixture into the tin. Put the tin in the fridge and chill for at least an hour.

⑨ Take the cake out of the tin. Put it onto a plate and peel off the foil or parchment. Cut it into squares or bars.

Sundaes

Berry sundae

Ingredients:

a large handful of mixed berries such as raspberries and strawberries

1 tablespoon of icing sugar

strawberry frozen yogurt or ice cream

vanilla frozen yogurt or ice cream

Makes one sundae

1. Set aside a few berries for decoration. Remove the stalks from the other strawberries, and cut them up. Put half the berries in a tall glass or sundae dish.

2. Put the rest of the berries in a bowl with the icing sugar and mash with a fork or a potato masher until it's smooth.

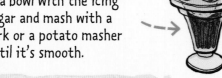

3. Scoop one ball of strawberry frozen yogurt or ice cream and one ball of vanilla. Put them in the dish. Pour over the berry sauce. Decorate with the berries you set aside.

Banana split

Ingredients:

1 ripe banana

2 tablespoons of cream cheese or mascarpone cheese

2 squares of chocolate

chocolate frozen yogurt or ice cream

vanilla frozen yogurt or ice cream

Makes one sundae

1. Put the cream cheese or mascarpone into a small pan and heat it gently for 5 minutes, until it melts. Take the pan off the heat and add the chocolate. Mix until the chocolate melts.

2. Leave the sauce to cool. Peel the banana and cut it in half. Put it in a shallow bowl or sundae dish.

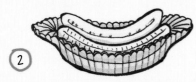

3. Scoop one ball of chocolate frozen yogurt or ice cream and one ball of vanilla. Put them in the dish, then drizzle over the sauce.

This banana split was made in a tall glass with extra yogurt and chopped nuts.

You could use canned fruit, such as pears, instead of fresh fruit.

You could make some chocolate curls by scraping a vegetable peeler across a bar of chocolate.

Look out for healthier frozen yogurts. These sundaes are also delicious if you use sorbets.

Add some other berries, such as blueberries, to your berry sundae.

Apple pie

Ingredients:

1 packet of ready-rolled shortcrust pastry (around 375g or 13oz)

1 lemon

5 eating apples

25g (1oz) granulated or caster sugar

2 pinches of ground cinnamon

a pinch of ground ginger

a little milk

This pie is quite large — you could invite some friends to eat it with you.

① Turn the oven to 200°C, 400°F or gas mark 6. Take the pastry out of the fridge, but leave it in its wrapper. Squeeze the juice from the lemon.

Make sure the knife is facing away from you.

② Cut the apples into quarters and cut out the cores. Then, peel the quarters.

③ Chop the apple into slices and put them into an ovenproof dish.

④ Sprinkle over the sugar, cinnamon, ginger and lemon juice and mix everything together with your hands.

⑤ Brush the edge of the dish with water. Unroll the pastry over the dish.

⑥ Press the pastry onto the dish rim with your thumbs. Cut off any extra pastry.

(7) Poke a hole in the pastry for steam to escape. Brush the pastry with some milk, then sprinkle over an extra spoonful of sugar.

(8) Bake for 10 minutes. Then, turn down the oven to 180°C, 350°F or gas mark 4 and bake for 25-30 minutes, until the pie is golden brown.

You could try...

...replacing half the apples with a couple of handfuls of blackberries, raspberries or blueberries

...or two cans of cherries in fruit juice. Drain well and add them instead of the apples at Step 4, leaving out the lemon juice

Apple pie is delicious eaten warm with custard.

Apple turnovers

If you don't have a pie dish, try making turnovers. Follow Steps 1-4 opposite, but mix the filling in a bowl instead of a pie dish. Then...

(1) Cut the pastry into 4 squares and pile the filling on one corner of each square.

(2) Brush the edges of each square with water and fold the pastry over to make a triangle. Pinch the edges together.

(3) Use a knife to cut a steam hole in each one, then brush with milk and sprinkle with sugar.

Bake at 200°C, 400°F or gas mark 6 for 20-25 minutes.

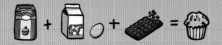

Choc chunk muffins

Ingredients:

a little butter

300g (10oz) self-raising flour

1½ teaspoons of baking powder

100g (4oz) caster sugar

200g (7oz) chocolate

This recipe makes 12 muffins.

100ml (4fl oz) sunflower oil

250ml (9fl oz) milk

1 egg

1 teaspoon of vanilla essence (optional)

① Heat your oven to 200°C, 400°F or gas mark 6. Cut a small chunk of butter and rub it all over the inside of a 12-hole muffin tray.

Chef's tips:

If you don't have a muffin tray, use a 20cm (8in) cake tin. Butter the inside, then follow Steps 2-5 of the muffin recipe.

Then, pour the muffin mixture into the cake tin. Bake for 20 minutes, then turn the oven down to 180°C, 350°F or gas mark 4 for another 15-20 minutes, until the cake is risen and brown.

② Put the flour, baking powder and sugar in a bowl. Break the chocolate into chunks and add them too.

③ Stir everything together, then make a hollow in the middle.

④ Measure the oil and milk in a jug. Break the egg into a bowl and beat it with a fork. Add it to the jug, with the vanilla essence.

For chocolatey muffin dough, add two tablespoons of cocoa powder at Step 2.

These muffins had a handful of fresh berries added at Step 2, too.

You could add some of these extra flavours to your muffins at Step 2...

...a handful of raisins or dried cranberries

...or a few chopped walnuts or hazelnuts

...or a teaspoon of finely grated lemon or orange rind

Make sure you measure out the ingredients carefully. If you use too much or too little of something, the muffins might go wrong.

The mixture will look a little lumpy.

⑤ Pour the oil and milk mixture into the hollow. Mix everything together with a fork. Don't stir too much, but make sure there are no pockets of flour left.

⑥ Spoon the mixture into the tray and put it in the oven. Bake for 20 minutes, until the muffins are risen and brown.

⑦ Leave them to cool in the tin for about ten minutes before you take them out.

Quick trifle

Berry trifle

Ingredients:

100g (4oz) bought plain cake

a little strawberry or raspberry jam

4 tablespoons of apple juice

225g (1/2lb) mixed berries such as strawberries and raspberries

1 tablespoon of granulated or caster sugar

5 tablespoons of cream cheese or mascarpone cheese

5 tablespoons of plain or Greek yogurt

1 teaspoon of vanilla extract (optional)

1. Cut the cake into slices. Spread half of them with jam, and place them at the bottom of a bowl. Put the rest of the cake on top.

2. Trickle the fruit juice over the top of the cake.

3. If you're using strawberries, pull out the green stalks. Cut them up if they are large.

4. Arrange the fruit on top of the cake. Sprinkle over the sugar. Then, make your trifle topping.

5. Put the cream cheese or mascarpone, the yogurt and the vanilla essence into a small bowl and mix together.

6. Spread the topping over the fruit. Put the trifle in the fridge for half an hour to let the cake soak up all the juice.

Orange and lemon trifle

Ingredients:

100g (4oz) bought lemon cake or plain cake

a little lemon curd or apricot jam

1 lemon

4 oranges

5 tablespoons of cream cheese or mascarpone cheese

5 tablespoons of plain or Greek yogurt

1 tablespoon of icing sugar

1. Cut the cake into slices. Spread half with the curd or jam, and place in a bowl. Put the rest of the cake on top.

2. Squeeze the juice from the lemon and one of the oranges. Mix the juice in a small bowl or jug. Trickle 4 tablespoons of the juice over the cake.

3. Peel the other oranges and cut them into small pieces. Put them on top of the cake.

4. Put the cream cheese or mascarpone, the yogurt, the sugar and one tablespoon of the juice into a small bowl. Mix, then follow Step 6 on the opposite page.

These individual trifles were made in small glasses and decorated with citrus rind.

Chef's tips:

Instead of buying cake, you could use a muffin from pages 60-61.

You could add a layer of custard or jelly before you spread on the topping. If you use jelly, follow the instructions on the packet, but don't try it with the orange and lemon trifle — the citrus juice will stop it setting.

Index